This gift is for

_____

From

_____

QUIET TIMES

TIMES

Uplifting Thoughts For Women

Janet M. Congo,
Julie L. Mask,
and Jan E. Meier

THOMAS NELSON PUBLISHERS
NASHVILLE

Published in Nashville, Tennessee, by Thomas Nelson, Inc., and distributed in Canada by Lawson Falle, Ltd., Cambridge, Ontario.

Unless otherwise indicated, Scripture quotations are from the NEW KING JAMES VERSION of the Bible. Copyright © 1979, 1980, 1982, Thomas Nelson, Inc., Publishers.

Scriptures marked NIV are from the Holy Bible, New International Version, copyright © 1973, 1978, 1984 International Bible Society. Used by permission of Zondervan Bible Publishers.

**Library of Congress
Cataloging-in-Publication Data**

See last page of book.

QUIET TIMES

That we may lead a quiet and peaceable life in all godliness and reverence.
—1 Tim. 2:2

What happens when we find the time to be quiet and listen? God's wisdom looms larger and our problems shrink. We must redecide daily to go to a quiet place where we can talk with God and meditate on His Word.

*L*ook at the birds of the air,
for they neither sow nor reap
nor gather into barns; yet
your heavenly Father feeds
them. Are you not of more
value than they?
—Matt. 6:26

When I see a storm raging I often wonder what will happen to the animals. After the storm, when I see the birds sing, I realize that God has not forsaken them. God will protect me, just as He protects the creatures of the earth.

And you will be sorrowful,
but your sorrow will be
turned to joy.
—John 16:20

*M*aterial things and kind words
are not all that is needed to mend a
wounded heart, or to replace a loss.
We must take the time to fully grieve
our loss. Then, and only then, can
we continue on with our lives
and find new joy.

By pride comes only
contention,
But with the well-advised
is wisdom.
—*Prov. 13:10*

$\mathcal{P}$ride exaggerates our strengths and denies our weaknesses. Love, however, frees us to be realistic about our strengths and honest about our weaknesses. Love is the effective—and healing—antidote to pride.

*Even a child is known
by his deeds,
Whether what he does
is pure and right.*
—Prov. 20:11

*W*hether our adolescents are failing in school, abusing drugs, or simply breaking rules, the most important thing we can do for them is allow them to accept responsibility for their actions.

*O*ur offenses and sins weigh
us down, and we are wasting
away because of them.
—*Ezek. 33:10* NIV

Too much garbage in our mind can push out all of the good things God wants to give us. Let's determine that today, with God's help, we will begin to make wise choices about what to do with the garbage that fills our minds.

Her children rise up and call her blessed; Her husband also, and he praises her.
—Prov. 31:28

While caring for your children, it is good to remember that they really will retain what you teach them. As you parent, pray for guidance to make wise decisions.

So then, my beloved brethren, let every man be swift to hear, slow to speak, slow to wrath.
—James 1:19

Just as we must train ourselves to listen to our loved ones on earth, we must train ourselves to listen to God. We must take the time to listen with our ears and our hearts and to look with our eyes at what God has done for us.

*Cast your burden
on the Lord,
And He shall sustain you;
He shall never permit the
righteous to be moved.
—Ps. 55:22*

I have had to learn to accept God's support through human support. As I have risked trusting, my load has become lighter, my understanding of God's love has deepened, and my acceptance of my humanity has increased.

All the paths of the Lord
are mercy and truth,
To such as keep His covenant
and His testimonies.
—Ps. 25:10

Often we hear easy, flippant praise of God's goodness. But God never promised us a rose garden; He just promised His presence. But His presence—His mercy and truth—is what can carry us through the bad times.

In a multitude of counselors
there is safety.
—Prov. 24:6

*Y*ou don't have to be alone. God has provided many wonderful people: friends, pastors, counsellors, who can support you as you go through life. Thank God for them.

*A*nd may the Lord make
you increase and abound in
love to one another and to all,
just as we do to you.
—1 Thess. 3:12

$\mathcal{H}$ave you ever failed at something important to you? To overcome feelings of shame, we may lash out at others. Shame is never healed by shaming someone else. Shame retreats in the face of love, grace, and acceptance.

*S*earch me, O God, and
know my heart;
Try me, and know
my anxieties.
—Ps. 139:23

$\mathcal{W}$e all have anxiety over our past and present circumstances. But eventually, we must come to terms with our situation, move on, and notice the pleasant things around us.

*The steps of a good man
are ordered by the Lord,
And He delights in his way.
—Ps. 37:23*

$\mathcal{W}$hen I set goals I think of small
steps that will help me reach that
goal. Small steps are better than no
steps. If you take a few small steps
every day you'll be at your
destination sooner
than you think.

*Your word is a lamp
to my feet
And a light to my path.
—Ps. 119:105*

Have you ever felt as if you had lost your way in life? God's Word is a light to our path. The more we immerse ourselves in God's Word, the more hope we will feel, even in seemingly hopeless situations.

God has spoken once, . . .
That power belongs to God.
—Ps. 62:11

Turning over our controlling tendencies to God can be a daily relief. Admitting we are powerless and that we need help from Jesus Christ places our lives in perspective.

Direct my steps by Your word,
And let no iniquity have
dominion over me.
—Ps. 119:133

$\mathcal{A}$nger is healthy when it protects good things. Anger can also protect things that are not good—like isolation and illusions. If your anger is protecting something that is not healthy, seek help to understand and process your anger.

*But it is good for me to
draw near to God;
I have put my trust
in the Lord GOD,
That I may declare
all Your works.*
—*Ps. 73:28*

God expects each of us to be responsible for establishing and maintaining a relationship with Him. He is pleased when we elect to become accountable for our own sins and to worship Him.

And He said to me, "My grace is sufficient for you, for My strength is made perfect in weakness."
—2 Cor. 12:9

$\mathcal{L}$ord, grant me the serenity to accept the things I cannot change, the courage to change the things I can, and the wisdom to know the difference.

A man has joy by the
answer of his mouth,
And a word spoken in due
season, how good it is!
—Prov. 15:23

*I*n our desire to establish a peaceful life, many of us have mistakenly learned to withhold our true thoughts. As we take the risk of relying on truth instead of pleasing others, we can rely on Christ to give us courage.

He gives power to the weak,
And to those who have
no might
He increases strength.
—Isa. 40:29

*R*ecovery feels like a dream in which we are trying to escape, but our body is stuck. In order for healing to take place, we must realize we are powerless and let God provide the daily power to walk through another battle.

$\mathcal{B}$ut as for me, I trust
in You, O Lord;
I say, "You are my God."
My times are in Your hand.
—Ps. 31:14–15

"Life is like a coin. You can spend it any way you want, but you can only spend it once." The choice of how we spend our time each day is one of the most important decisions we will make in life.

Fear not, for I am with you;
Be not dismayed, for I
am your God.
—Isa. 41:10

$\mathcal{S}$olitude and loneliness are two very different things. Solitude helps acquaint us with who we are and who God is. Loneliness causes us to feel isolated and sad. As we cultivate solitude, we must also develop a plan to avoid loneliness.

*W*ho shall separate us from
the love of Christ?
—Rom. 8:35

So many of us feel as if God were distant. The truth is that He hasn't moved. He looks at us with eyes of love and compassion—with no condemnation in His gaze. Why not bask in the warmth of His love and acceptance today?

*T*he Lord has appeared of
old to me, saying:
"Yes, I have loved you with an
everlasting love;
Therefore with lovingkindness
I have drawn you."
—Jer. 31:3

I often wonder if God sometimes laughs at our futile attempts to earn love. Then He just loves and accepts us for who we are and asks that we love in the same way.

But when Jesus heard that, He said to them, "Those who are well have no need of a physician, but those who are sick."
—Matt. 9:12

$\mathcal{N}$eeds are the fuel for growth.
Thank you Lord for my neediness.

Better to dwell in
the wilderness,
Than with a contentious
and angry woman.
—Prov. 21:19

*A*nger mixed with denial is a deadly twosome. It may result in a person who goes around like a bomb, ready to explode. If you have a tendency to "blow up" over small matters, look for the true source of your anger.

*A*nd He said to them, "Go into all the world and preach the gospel to every creature."
—Mark 16:15

$\mathcal{A}$s God's love transforms us and puts us together, we affect our world. That is what ministry is all about. Even though our words are important, what we are speaks louder than what we say.

For as he thinks in his heart, so is he.
—*Prov. 23:7*

*S*elf-defeating thought cycles can be broken, but only if the heart is touched at an emotional and thinking level. And that happens if, every day, we dedicate our minds and our thoughts to Jesus.

And above all things have fervent love for one another, for "love will cover a multitude of sins."
—*1 Peter 4:8*

$\mathcal{M}$any of us are in marriages
that take a great amount of work.
But we frequently get so caught up
in working on the weaknesses in the
relationship that we forget the joy
and contentment we share.
Encourage one another.

If we say that we have no sin, we deceive ourselves.
—1 John 1:8

*I*t takes arrogance for a person to believe she is either the worst sinner or the best saint in the world. Humility is the key for the black-white thinker. We must realize that we are all sinners saved by grace.

I will praise You, for I am fearfully and wonderfully made; Marvelous are Your works, And that my soul knows very well.
—Ps. 139:13

*I*t took me many years to make this verse mine. Finally, I acknowledged that I was a unique creation of the unique God of the universe—a divine original. God isn't finished with me yet. But that's OK—I'm not finished either.

Therefore I say to you, do not worry about your life, what you will eat or what you will drink; nor about your body, what you will put on. Is not life more than food and the body more than clothing?
—Matt. 6:25

The only things of value in life are relationships we have with Jesus and with those around us. If we spent as much time on these two areas as we do on satisfying our food and material appetites, we would live in abundance.

*The Lord is my light and
my salvation;
Whom shall I fear?
The Lord is the strength
of my life;
Of whom shall I be afraid?*
—Ps. 27:1

Fear comes in many forms. When moments of fear come, how do we respond? One helpful response is to join the psalmist in affirming,

"I will fear no evil;
For You are with me (Ps. 23:4b)."

Because, although they knew God, they did not glorify Him as God, nor were thankful, but became futile in their thoughts, and their foolish hearts were darkened.
—Rom. 1:21

$\mathcal{M}$any of us persist in believing that happiness will be just over the next hill. But happiness is not a destination; it is a journey. Don't brood over what would make you happy tomorrow. Instead, be grateful for today.

*Let the words of my mouth
and the meditation
of my heart
Be acceptable in Your sight,
O Lord, my strength
and my redeemer.*
—Ps. 19:14

God loves us and wants the best for us. The more we accept ourselves, the more at peace we feel. The greatest thing about believing God thinks we are valuable is being able to help others see that about themselves.

*N*ow may the God of
patience and comfort grant
you to be like-minded toward
one another, according
to Christ Jesus.
—Rom. 15:5

God has such patience with us, and we have so little patience with ourselves. Yet patience is a part of accepting who we are and being satisfied with how we have been created—as growing individuals with whom God is not yet finished.

For You, O God, have
proved us;
You have refined us as silver
is refined.
—Ps. 66:10

$\mathcal{W}$e can refine ourselves on a daily basis by opening ourselves to self-examination, asking God to reveal areas that need improvement. May our growth come from a daily, Christ-guided process of refinement.

And let us not grow weary while doing good, for in due season we shall reap if we do not lose heart.
—Gal. 6:9

$\mathcal{G}$od made each of us unique, and His goal for us is to become the best we can be—not like everyone else. He wants us to be like Christ, secure in our mission and secure in the One who sent us on that mission.

*A*nd we know that all things
work together for good to
those who love God.
—Rom. 8:28

*W*hatever the reason bad things happen, here is a truth we can rely on: God can bring good out of bad. We can also be sure that God loves us. He will help us overcome—not be overcome by—our problems in life.

*N*ow godliness with
contentment is great gain.
—1 Tim. 6:6

$\mathcal{L}$eading our life in a manner that contributes to the welfare of ourselves and others is what contentment is about, and it is our faith rather than life experiences that produces true contentment.

Speaking the truth in love.
—Eph. 4:15

$\mathcal{W}$hen you talk, is the other person touched by your acceptance, understanding, empathy, and truth? The only person who lived "truth in love" perfectly was Jesus Christ. Let's ask His help with our communication.

God is able to make all
grace abound toward you, that
you . . . may have an
abundance for every
good work.
—2 Cor. 9:8

Think about the areas in your life where you are in need of help. Now relax in the assurance that Jesus' grace will always be there for you—ready when you need it.

It is vain for you to
rise up early,
To sit up late.
—Ps. 127:2

$\mathcal{R}$est is so important for human beings that God made it the basis of the Fourth Commandment. When we don't rest, little issues become big issues, and problems mount. That's why our Lord tells us to get some rest.

*Talk no more so
very proudly;
Let no arrogance come
from your mouth,
For the Lord is the God
of knowledge;
And by Him actions
are weighed.
—1 Sam. 2:3*

*I*f we respect intelligence as a gift from our Lord, we will not be prideful about it. And knowledge is pleasing to the Lord when we use it to glorify Him, and serve others, not when we pride ourselves in it.

Library of Congress
Cataloging-in-Publication Data

Congo, Janet.
  Quiet times / Janet M. Congo, Julie L. Mask,
and Jan E. Meier.
      p.   cm.
  ISBN 0-8407-7813-9
  1. Women—Prayer-books and devotions—
English. 2. Christian life—1960–   I. Mask,
Julie. II. Meier, Jan. III. Title.
BV4527.C6437 1993
242'.643—dc20   92-37890
                                        CIP

Printed in Singapore.
1 2 3 4 5 6 7 — 96 95 94 93